The butterfly is a symbol that witnesses to newness of life and growth in Christ.

Freedom and beauty are associated with the butterfly, as they are with the Christian who embraces the gospel in its fullness.

Stretching and Growing

and

Growing

By Charles R. Shumate

A Guide
for the
New Christian

WARNER
Press

Anderson, Indiana

© 1997 by Warner Press
ISBN # 0-87162-811-2   Stock # D-9001
UPC # 7-3081721850-2

All rights reserved
Printed in the United States of America
Warner Press, Inc

David C. Shultz, Editor in Chief
Holly D. Miller, Editor
Arthur Kelly, Managing Editor
Cover and Layout by
    Curtis D. Corzine and Virginia L. Wachenschwanz

Contents

WELCOME,
TO THE FAMILY OF GOD!

You are a special person! You are special because God knows you are special. Recently you claimed your place ... you lifted your hands in the air, bent your knees to the ground, and accepted Jesus Christ as your Lord.

Now what?

That's where this guidebook can help. The ten chapters contained between the covers of this small book are the "what's next" in your personal journey of becoming a Christian. But before you begin, you need to understand that this journey is never-ending ... that Christians are *always* becoming. The gifted scholar, the serious theologian, the dedicated Bible-study teacher, and the life-long church member never stop stretching, growing, having new insights, and finding fresh ways to apply their faith. So, welcome. You are already part of the family.

As you work through the stretching exercises at the end of each chapter, you might want to jot down your thoughts in a journal. Or, you might set aside extra time to think about the ideas that will come to you. Some people like to memorize passages of scripture that illustrate the lessons they learn; others respond by paraphrasing the verses, using contemporary language and examples to make the words more meaningful. Your options are practically endless.

However you choose to use this book, begin each study session with a prayer. Ask God for understanding. At some point you may feel ready to share your new faith with friends who are contemplating faith journeys of their own.

My personal prayer for you is that these pages may encourage you to stretch and grow in your exciting new relationship with Jesus Christ.

Charles R. Shumate
Church Extension and Home Missions
Church Growth Ministries

Chapter 1

What it means
to be saved

Y ou've heard the expression, "God moves in mysterious ways." As a newcomer to the faith, perhaps you've been tempted to add: And Christians rely on mysterious clichés!

People of faith often seem to converse in a language all their own. They're likely to share their "testimony" with you, recount the moment when they were "saved," talk about having "assurance," and marvel at being "filled with the Holy Spirit." They embrace you and your "decision for Christ" and celebrate the fact that you, too, have been "saved."

Confused by all this jargon? Are you uncertain as to whether you've been saved *from* something or saved *for* something?

> If you confess with your mouth, "Jesus is Lord," and believe in your heart that God raised him from the dead, you will be saved.
>
> —Romans 10:9, NIV

This is God's assurance that if you believe in Jesus and have faith in the gospel, salvation is yours. But God doesn't save you merely to take you to heaven. He wants your love, allegiance, and sacrifice while you are here on earth. You have been saved for a purpose, and that purpose is to share your new life in service to Jesus Christ. A relationship to Jesus, described in John 15, is similar to that of a branch and a vine. You are connected to Jesus; your life depends on him. You've exchanged your old existence for a new one. You've become a new person, as surely as if you have been "born again"—another favorite expression in the Christian vocabulary.

The Bible also says, "Believe in the Lord Jesus, and you will be saved" (Acts 16:31). This passage sounds easy enough until you consider its implications. The verse is asking you to believe in something that you can neither see nor touch. To believe is to have faith, and faith is sometimes discounted as silly sentimentalism or murky mysticism in this age of research, evidence, facts, and proof "beyond a shadow of a doubt."

THE MEANING AND NATURE OF FAITH

Read this statement and decide if it is true: "Xdsr xm lkkf ssddkfe nxr, xmz, mckjh, hicaroutu, mpkffge." Your reply, naturally, is "I don't know what you said. How can I believe that the statement is true when I can't understand it?" Here is an essential ingredient of true faith. If you are to believe that something is true, you must know what that something is. You may not understand all aspects of it, but you must know something about it.

Many people say they believe in God, but when asked what they believe about God, they have no reply. Their faith has no content.

Saving faith says, "I have put aside all else, ... in order that I can have Christ, and become one with him, no longer counting on being saved by being good enough ... but by trusting Christ to save me; for God's way of making us right with himself depends on faith—counting on Christ alone" (Phil 3:8–9, THE LIVING BIBLE).

You can't truly believe in Christianity without a knowledge of the gospel and a familiarity with the teachings of Christ. At the heart of the Christian faith is the good news of eternal life in Jesus Christ. You are a Christian if you have heard the good news and received Christ by inviting him into your life, asking him to forgive you of your sins. A second consideration is that you also must see applications for Christ's teachings in your life. Only when you feel connected to your Savior in every aspect of your daily routine will you know that you have a personal, meaningful relationship with Jesus Christ.

THE LOVE CONNECTION

Some people are confused today as to the most important component of the Christian life. They argue that to have a correct theology or doctrine is essential. The Pharisees were classic examples of this type of religious followers. They were very concerned about rules of conduct. Social and political correctness were their specialties. Often their hearts were filled with intolerance toward other people because they hadn't discovered that the most important aspect of a person's life can be summed up in one word: "love." Jesus tells us to love one another, and the apostle Paul repeats the lesson in 1 Corinthians, "If I speak in the tongues of men and of angels, but have not love, I am only a resounding gong or a clanging cymbal" (1 Corinthians 13:1, NIV).

The expression of love is positive proof that you have been saved and that you believe in Jesus Christ. John 13:34–35 says, "A new commandment I give to you, that you love one another; even as I have loved you, that you also love one another. By this all (people) will know that you are my disciples" (RSV).

Faithful Christian believers—people who have been saved—are easily recognized by the love they exhibit for one another.

Stretching Exercises

Faith is a word you have heard—and used—thousands of times. But what does it mean to you? Without checking a dictionary, try to define it. Or, if a definition is difficult, think of an example when someone you know displayed faith.

Consider the passage from Matthew 1:21 that says, "she will bear a son, and you shall call his name Jesus, for he will save his people from their sins" (RSV).

Paraphrase this promise _____

_____

_____

_____

_____

Do you believe this is true? _____

_____

_____

_____

If you believe that Jesus came to save the "sinner," did he also come to save you? Are you among the "sinners?"

_____

_____

_____

_____

_____

Read these words of assurance in Isaiah 1:18, "Come now, and let us reason together," says Jehovah. "Though your sins be as scarlet, they shall be as white as snow; though they be red like crimson, they shall be as wool" (KJV). Rewrite the verse in your own words.

_____

_____

_____

_____

_____

_____

Is God speaking to you with these words? If you have had a special experience of peace, joy, contentment, or deliverance, write about it in your journal.

As you think about the "new commandment" that Jesus gave us in the gospel of John—"love one another, even as I have loved you"—try to identify three specific actions you might take in your personal life that would express love toward your family. Now consider ways you might express love on the job, in your volunteer or community life, and among your friends and colleagues.

At home	**On the job**
_____	_____
_____	_____
_____	_____
_____	_____

As you learn more about Jesus through daily prayer and Bible study, you may begin to make subtle changes in your life. Perhaps you'll feel that God is leading you away from old habits and toward a new kind of lifestyle. Trace your

Stretching and Growing

growth by first making note of the way that God made his will known to you; jot down the adjustments that you believe God wants you to make in your life; finally, record the adjustments that you have made.

God's Word spoke to me ...

_____

_____

_____

Adjustments God wants me to make in my life include ...

_____

_____

_____

_____

Adjustments I have made since accepting Jesus include ...

_____

_____

_____

_____

Journal

Chapter 2

How to use
the scriptures

Imagine for a moment that a friend has asked you three questions pertaining to the Bible. First, he or she wants to hear your explanation of what it is. You respond quickly, "It's the Word of God," and then you embellish your answer with a few superlatives. "It's the greatest book ever written, the best seller of all times, and a collection of sixty-six books all bound together in one magnificent volume," you exude. And you're right.

Your friend's next question requires a bit more thought. "Exactly what is in the Bible?" the friend asks.

"Two major sections," you reply with confidence. "There's the Old Testament, which traces the interactions of God with the Hebrew people. These thirty-nine books let the reader know how the Hebrews lived and worshiped. On a more important level, the Old Testament contains the promises that God revealed through a handful of carefully chosen prophets. Christians generally view this collection of ancient books as a record of how God prepared his people for the coming of Jesus Christ."

"Which leads to the New Testament," you continue. "These twenty-seven books show the fulfillment of the Old Testament's promises and prophecies. They tell the story of Christ's birth, ministry, death, and resurrection, and include his famous challenge to his disciples to go into the world and spread his message. In fact, Christians still follow this 'great commission' by talking about Jesus with people who may not know him."

Now comes your friend's toughest question. "Okay, you've told me what the Bible is, and you've told me what's in it," she or he says. "Now explain what's in it for me."

GOOD BOOK OR GOD'S BOOK?

Unless you can honestly articulate what's in the Bible for you, then this "greatest book ever written" is little more than another best seller, an interesting history of other times, other places, and other people. It lacks relevance. It's a good book but not God's book. It's a quirky compilation of teachings, lessons, and sayings that may seem out of touch with a world on the brink of the twenty-first century. Unless you relate to the Bible on an everyday basis and on a personal level, it comes up short when compared with the scores of self-help books produced each year by modern Christian authors.

The Bible is much more than another religious resource. Second Timothy 3:16 says, "All Scripture is God-breathed and is useful for teaching, rebuking, correcting, and training in righteousness" (NIV). God-breathed? This means that God breathed life into it. While you might be strengthened by the concepts and illustrations presented in contemporary books, you read the Bible to learn directly from your heavenly Father. He gave it to you to teach and encourage you as you grow in your new faith.

For many new Christians, the Bible doesn't seem "reader friendly." So many pages! they complain. So many names that are impossible to pronounce! They assume that the obvious place to begin their study is with the phrase "In the beginning...." They think—wrongly so—that they are expected to absorb the Bible in sequence, from Genesis to Revelation.

FIRST: THE GOSPELS

While the whole Bible is important in the life and growth of the individual, the gospels constitute the primary lens through which the believer views the entire Bible. Since this is so, as a new Christian, consider beginning with Matthew, Mark, Luke, and John. Start with them, but not necessarily in that order. Choose Mark as your first reading assignment because it is written as a narrative, is full of action, and is simpler and more direct than the other three. It vividly tells the story of Jesus.

Read the entire Book of Mark at one sitting. This will take about an hour and a quarter if you read it aloud and much less if you read it silently. After Mark, work your way through Luke and notice how the author stresses the availability of salvation for all people. Read Matthew next and be aware of the emphasis on Jesus as a teacher. Finally, in John, you'll recognize the seven signs that point to Jesus as the Son of God.

As you continue your reading program, select the shorter letters written by Paul, such as Ephesians and Philippians, and then read the opening eight chapters of Romans. By this time you will be familiar enough with the New Testament to make your own selections. Before long, you'll be ready to turn to Genesis and learn what it was like "In the beginning...."

Stretching Exercises

Do not merely listen to the word, and so deceive yourselves. Do what it says. Anyone who listens to the word but does not do what it says is like a man who looks at his face in a mirror and, after looking at himself, goes away and immediately forgets what he looks like.

—James 1:22–23, NIV

This passage suggests that for the Bible to have application in your life, you need to interact with it as you read it. Here are a couple of ways to do this:

√ Read a passage from the Bible and then ask yourself a question that has five parts. The question and its parts are easy to remember if you think of the acronym SPACE. Here's the question: Does the scripture that I just read bring to mind any

Sins I should confess?
Promises I should claim?
Actions I should take?
Commandments I should obey?
Examples I should follow?

Write your reactions to these questions in your journal. From your responses, identify a specific commandment that you want to follow, attach an action that you plan to take that is based on the commandment, and include an example from the Bible that illustrates the action and the commandment.

WHICH BIBLE DO I USE?

√ Personalize a scripture passage by inserting your name into it. For example, slightly alter James 1:22–23 so it advises, "If Mary Jones merely listens to the word, she will deceive herself. Mary needs to do what it says. If Mary listens but does not act, it is as if she looks at her face in the mirror and, after seeing herself, she goes away and immediately forgets what she looks like."

Plan to visit a Christian bookstore or the library at a seminary or Christian college. Take time to thoroughly familiarize yourself with the various translations of the Bible that are available. If you plan to buy a new Bible, you want to make sure that you choose one that is readable and understandable for you. You don't want a version that you will "outgrow" because it is too simplistic and conversational; at the same time, you don't want a version that is so academic that you constantly must consult footnotes or a commentary to comprehend it.

The International Bible Society suggests a sensible way to determine which Bible is right for you: Choose a couple of scriptures that you know well—perhaps the 23rd Psalm or the first few passages of Genesis—and read several translations of these verses. Notice how some versions are very contemporary, while some rely on ancient word forms. Read the passages out loud. You may find that the modern translations don't flow as well as the traditional translations,

You may be distracted or even stumble over the "thee's," and "thou's," and "yea, verily's" of early translations, however.

Now choose a couple of unfamiliar passages and read several versions of them out loud. Are you able to grasp the meaning? Often we understand familiar verses, regardless of the translation, because we have heard them so often. A less familiar text may be a better indicator of readability.

Regardless of the Bible translation that you choose, a good way to begin each reading is by affirming the authority of the scriptures. Among the many verses that will remind you of the power and importance of the Bible is Hebrews 1:1–2. "In the past God spoke to our forefathers through the prophets at many times and in various ways, but in these last days he has spoken to us by his Son ..." (NIV).

Journal

Chapter 3

Pray as you go:
daily devotions

Prayer isn't an option for a Christian, it's a necessity—a lifeline to God. Prayer strengthens and guides you as you wrestle with difficult decisions, endure periods of discouragement, and fight the temptations that are so much a part of life.

Think about the unusual characteristics of prayer. It is *portable.* No matter where you are or what circumstances surround you, prayer is there for the asking. It goes with you to work, can be called on during a confrontation, is available as you sit at the bedside of a sick friend, and can rejuvenate you for the next task on your to-do list.

Prayer is also *personal.* There is no single, universal way to pray. Like the dialogue between two special friends, the communication that occurs between you and God is unique. It addresses your concerns, your day, your feelings, your relationship with your heavenly father.

Prayer is very *private.* Someone once injected humor in the ongoing argument about prayer in public school. The observer stated that "as long as there are tests in public schools, there will be prayer in public schools." It's true! You can pray silently and fervently in a roomful of people without anyone's knowledge. You can shut the door on the busyness of the world, retreat into prayer, and ask for guidance, strength, humility, and patience. (Jesus said, "When you pray, go into your room, close the door and pray to your Father, who is unseen.")

Finally, prayer is *powerful.* How often the Bible assures us of the power of prayer.

√ I have heard thy prayer, I have seen thy tears: behold, I will heal thee.

(2 Kings 20:5, KJV)

17

√ Whosoever shall call on the name of the Lord shall be delivered.

(Joel 2:32, KJV)

√ Every one that asketh receiveth.

(Matthew 7:8, Luke 11:10, KJV)

GUIDELINES FOR DAILY DEVOTIONS

As you continue to stretch and grow in Christ, you will discover the importance of setting aside time for daily devotions. Perhaps you'll prefer the early morning when the house is quiet. Or maybe the evening will be best, right before bedtime. As you experiment with times and places for private worship, consider these seven guidelines.

Commit to a time.

Our English word *devotion* comes from a Latin term that means "to vow" or "to promise." A daily devotion is a time that you have set aside and promised to spend with God in worship. Think of it as a standing appointment that is important because someone is waiting for you. And be assured—God is.

Choose a place.

Few of us are fortunate enough to have a room we can set aside solely for devotional worship. Typically, your worship center also doubles as dining room, laundry room or den. Use your creativity to evoke a different mood so you won't be distracted by thoughts of the activities usually associated with the room. Light a small candle, add an arrangement of garden flowers, or pop a tape of soft inspirational music into your headset.

Talk with God.

Imagine Jesus sitting in a chair near you or standing beside you with a hand on your shoulder. Now, talk with him as you would talk with a very intimate friend. Don't feel obligated to use archaic words—thee and thou—or conjure up flowery language that is alien to you. Engage in direct and candid dialogue.

Listen quietly.

Why does silence make us uncomfortable? Why do we feel the need to "keep the conversation going" by chattering idly? Prayer time isn't a monologue but a dialogue. Don't monopolize the conversation with bloated phrases and wordy prayers. Stop talking and listen to what God is saying to you. Respect his wisdom, and pray that he will share that wisdom with you. Then, give him time—quiet time—to answer your prayer.

Read scripture.

Often God will speak to you by giving you insights as you read the Bible. Unlike the scholarly research you may do as part of a Bible study group, the scripture reading you do during your daily devotions is more to inspire than to educate. God inspired the Bible (translated: God breathed in his spirit) so that you will be inspired by it.

Anticipate or review your day.

Depending on the time of your devotions, you may want to anticipate the events of the day or review those events. Someone once said that each day is a gift from God, and that is why it is called "the present." Ask yourself, what will I (or, what did I) do with this "present" from God? Pray for his help as you look ahead to a difficult situation on your agenda, or ask for his peace as you put the day's events behind you.

Close with praise.

You will probably find that you will feel relaxed, fortified, or replenished after your daily devotions. Thank God for this by ending on a note of praise. Perhaps you have found an appropriate verse in the Bible that summarizes your feeling. "From the rising of the sun unto the going down of the same the LORD'S name *is* to be praised" (Psalm 113:3, KJV). Or, you might repeat a doxology (any brief expression of praise to God) that you've sung in church.

Stretching Exercises

If communicating with God is difficult for you, try to identify obstacles to prayer and then design strategies to overcome them. Sometimes the barriers are external—not enough time, no quiet place, too many interruptions, a stressful schedule that seems overwhelming. And sometimes they are internal—feelings of anger, guilt or envy that preoccupy you and rob you of your time with your heavenly father. Be creative as you determine how you are going to surmount the obstacles.

Obstacles	Strategies
_____	_____
_____	_____
_____	_____
_____	_____

One of the best known verses in the Bible is Matthew 7:7: "Ask and it will be given you; seek, and you will find; knock, and it will be opened to you" (RSV). What do these words mean to you? How would you paraphrase them?

_____

_____

_____

How would you respond to the skeptic who asks, "Does this mean that a Christian can create a wish list and be assured of receiving every item on the list?"

_____

_____

_____

21

Prayer is two-way communication. Not only do we communicate with God through our words and our thoughts, but we also hear from him. Think about a time when you've been in prayer and God has communicated with you by giving you a special insight that has helped you solve a problem or deal with a difficult situation.

Try to recall the details as you write in your journal:

_____
_____
_____

How God's Word spoke to me during prayer ...

_____
_____
_____

Adjustments that I have felt God wants in my life ...

_____
_____

Adjustments I have made after communicating with God in prayer ...

_____
_____
_____

Journal

Chapter 4

Blessed assurance

Have you ever noticed that mature Christians—people who have been in the faith for a long time—have a wonderful serenity about them? They seem to radiate an inner peace, and no matter what kind of difficult situation they face, they never lose their calmness. They don't second guess what is happening to them, they don't ask "why me?" or "what if?" questions, and they aren't plagued by doubts about the future. They know that God has a plan for them, and they wait in anticipation—not in fear—as it unfolds.

Serenity comes from feeling secure, safe, and loved. We can't know true contentment until we are convinced in our hearts that we are the children of God, that he is in control of our lives, that he loves us in spite of the mistakes we make, and that he will always take care of us. Once that blessed assurance comes, we, too, can know the joy of inner peace and outer calmness.

Jesus, the Prince of Peace, promised us the gift of inner peace before he was crucified. "Peace I leave with you; my peace I give you. I do not give to you as the world gives. Do not let your hearts be troubled and do not be afraid," he told his disciples in John 14:27, (NIV).

Feeling the assurance of God's love is essential as you stretch and grow in your faith. Here are two reasons to actively seek out and pray for this assurance:

√ Without it, you cannot fully enjoy the Christian life. If you feel uncertain about your relationship with God, if you experience unrest, uncertainty, or dissatisfaction about your experience with him, you will be distracted from your task of serving as a witness for Christ.

√ When you have felt the convicting power of the Holy Spirit, and you have asked forgiveness for your sins and turned to Christ, you can speak with force as you tell others about your faith. You become a strong and believable witness for Christ.

Seeking Assurance Daily

Sometimes assurance comes quickly and easily; other times it comes slowly and requires much prayer and meditation. The good news is that you can build up your feelings of certainty and assurance by following three simple guidelines.

First, cultivate your growing faith in Christ. You know you have turned from sin and have given yourself wholly to God. Keep thanking him for what he has done for you.

Second, follow Christ's example by leading a life of obedience and service. Good feelings spring from a life of commitment.

Third, be faithful in your daily devotions. Read the Bible, develop habits of daily prayer and communion with Christ. Meet with Christians whose lives inspire you, talk with them, and pray with them. You will find your relationship with God growing deeper. Without thinking about assurance, you will find your heart abundantly secure in the knowledge that God is in control.

As part of your daily devotions, try to find verses that address this whole concept of assurance although they may not refer to it by that name. Here are a few passages to get you started:

√ By this we know that we abide in him and he in us, because he has given us of his own Spirit (1 John 4:13, RSV).

√ It is the Spirit himself bearing witness with our spirit that we are children of God, and if children, then heirs, heirs of God and fellow heirs with Christ (Romans 8:16–17, RSV).

√ He who believes in the Son of God has the testimony [witness] in himself (1 John 5:10, RSV).

√ But I am not ashamed, for I know whom I have believed, and I am sure that he is able to guard until that Day what has been entrusted to me (2 Timothy 1:12, RSV).

√ If any one is in Christ, he is a new creation; the old has passed away, behold, the new has come (2 Corinthians 5:17, RSV).

√ Therefore, since we are justified by faith, we have peace with God through our Lord Jesus Christ.... we rejoice in our hope of sharing the glory of God (Romans 5:1–2, RSV).

√ As a hart (deer) longs for flowing streams, so longs my soul for thee, O God (Psalm 42 1–2a, RSV).

THE PROMISE OF TRANQUILITY

The 23rd Psalm, one of the best known and loved portions of the Bible, serves as a model of the tranquility that is possible when someone feels assured of God's love. This is particularly obvious if you add a few words at the beginning and at the end of David's psalm: "(Because) the LORD is my shepherd, I shall not be in want." And the closing says: "(I have assurance that) goodness and love will follow me all the days of my life, and I will dwell in the house of the Lord forever"(NIV)

How can you achieve this tranquility? Jesus provides us with the most direct answer: "For God so loved the world that he gave his one and only Son, that whoever believes in him shall not perish but have eternal life" (John 3:16, NIV).

Stretching Exercises

Jesus told his disciples that "I do not give to you (peace) as the world gives" (John 14:27, NIV). What do you think he meant by this? How is worldly peace different from spiritual peace? Paraphrase his assurance here:

_____

_____

_____

_____

_____

_____

Think of a very secure relationship that you enjoy with a family member. List the characteristics of that relationship. For example, it is based on love? Respect? Do you feel comfortable telling that special person your deepest fears and regrets? Can you call on that person any time, day or night? Do you refrain from judging each other but, instead, support each other no matter what happens? Now, review your list and put a check by every characteristic that also describes your relationship with Jesus Christ.

In your journal, try to recall moments when you felt sure of God's presence and love. Was the moment marked by a sense of inner peace and tranquility? Or, did you feel energized and empowered?

If you are like many new Christians, you feel most secure in God's love during times of quiet prayer. Plan to spend fifteen minutes in prayer early every morning. Broaden your conversation with God by focusing on different aspects of your relationship.

√ Dedication. You are already dedicated to God; now renew that dedication with a vow to walk more closely by his side.

√ Adoration. Think about the greatness of God and the wonder of his ability to hear each one of us.

√ Thanksgiving. Review all the mercies and miracles in your life. They are more plentiful than you may suspect. Thank him for health, home, love, work, friends, books, fun, a night's rest.

√ Guidance. Ask God for guidance all day long. Preview your day. Imagine each task that is in store for you. Plan to complete it together.

√ Intercession. Pray for others. Have a prayer list and add to it regularly. Ask for God's mercy on everyone from world leaders to the children in your neighborhood.

√ Petition. Prayers should never consist of a laundry list of blessings and creature comforts that we think will make us happy. Certainly we can ask for Christ's touch during an illness. But instead of requesting solutions to all our problems, why not pray for the strength to bear the burden of the problems?

√ Meditation. Conclude your prayer as you began it—with meditation. Think quietly but deeply about wisdom, joy, love, beauty, light, peace, power, freedom, and holiness.

Chapter 5

You and the Holy Spirit

Although the words "Holy Trinity" never appear in the Bible, most of us understand them to mean the Father, Son, and Holy Spirit. We know that the Father is God; the Son of God is Jesus Christ; but who or what is the Holy Spirit? Jesus never defines the Holy Spirit, but helps us understand that the Holy Spirit is known best by what the Spirit does in us, around us, and through us. He likens the Spirit to the wind—invisible, powerful, and can't be directed or controlled by human beings.

Like the wind, the Holy Spirit lets us know—through our senses of sight, touch, and hearing—where the Spirit is and has been. We can't see the Spirit, but we can see evidence of his presence. We know the Spirit exists because he envelops, cools, and warm us. Gentle or strong, comforting or frightening—Jesus describes the Holy Spirit this way:

> The wind blows where it wills, and you hear the sound of it, but you do not know whence it comes or whither it goes; so it is with every one who is born of the Spirit.
>
> —John 3:8, RSV

In the Old Testament (Joel 2:28–32), God explains what happens to people when he pours his Spirit onto and into them. We learn that the Spirit empowers them, enables them to have visions and dreams of the future, and allows them to see and understand the wonders in the heavens.

Later, in the New Testament (Acts 1:1–11 and Acts 2), Jesus describes this pouring out of the Spirit as "the gift my Father promised." The gift is delivered to the disciples on Pentecost, and again, the image of the wind is used to describe the sound that came from heaven and filled the place where the disciples had gathered. When they received their gift—"all of them were filled with the Holy Spirit"—they suddenly had abilities and talents they never had before. They realized that although Jesus was no longer with them in the flesh, he was with them through the presence of the Holy Spirit in their hearts. They knew now that Jesus had come back to them in the person of the Holy Spirit, and they were aware of his power to work within and through them. They were empowered to carry on the ministry of Jesus, just as he taught them.

GROWING IN THE SPIRIT

Many new Christians recall with great detail the first time they felt the Holy Spirit stirring in them. For some people, the moment was dramatic and was characterized by a "washing over" sensation. For others, the feeling was more subtle, better described as a "welling up" sensation. The first seemed external; the second was internal.

As you continue to grow in your faith, you will feel the Holy Spirit become a stronger, more powerful force in your life. For example, Jesus says that the Holy Spirit will work on your conscience and heart to help you recognize and resist sin. Your sense of right and wrong will become sharper. In some translations of the Bible, the Holy Spirit is referred to as "Counselor," which suggests that the Spirit will offer you wisdom when you wrestle with difficult choices. As you read God's word and pray for guidance, the Holy Spirit will give you the power to shrug off temptation and remain firm in your convictions.

Just as the Holy Spirit assumes the role of counselor, so does he serve as teacher. As you grow more knowledgeable of the scriptures, the Holy Spirit will give you insights and help you make connections between the Old and New Testaments. You will see how the lessons contained in the Bible apply to your life today. Jesus assures us that "the Holy Spirit, whom the Father will send in my name, he will teach you all things, and bring to your remembrance all that I have said to you" (John 14:26, RSV).

Stretching Exercises

Sometimes the Bible refers to the Holy Spirit by other names. For example, in the King James translation, Jesus talks of the Spirit as the "Comforter." In John 14:16, he explains, "The Father ... shall give you another Comforter, that he may abide with you for ever." Later, in John 16:7, Jesus says, "If I go not away, the Comforter will not come unto you." If the Father gives the disciples a second Comforter, who was the first Comforter? Why couldn't this second Comforter come to them while Jesus was still on earth? Paraphrase what you think these passages mean.

_____

_____

_____

The Bible lists the fruits of the Spirit as love, joy, peace, patience, kindness, goodness, faithfulness, gentleness, and self-control. Think about your own experience in becoming a Christian and the changes that have occurred since you made your commitment. Complete these sentences.

I first felt the stirring of the Holy Spirit in me when ...

_____

_____

Since the Holy Spirit came into my life, I have experienced the following positive changes ...

_____

_____

As the Holy Spirit grows stronger in me, I feel God wants me to

_____

_____

We all have special gifts, given to us by the Spirit, to be used in spreading the gospel of Jesus. The Bible assures us that, "to each one the manifestation of the Spirit is given for the common good. To one there is given through the Spirit the message of wisdom, to another the message of knowledge by means of the same Spirit, to another faith by the same Spirit, to another gifts of healing by that one Spirit, to another miraculous powers, to another prophecy ..." (1 Corinthians 12:7–10, NIV). List your special gifts on the left; then, on the right, jot down how you might use those gifts "for the common good."

Gifts from the Spirit   **Ways to use the gifts**

_____   _____
_____   _____
_____   _____
_____   _____

Meditation: As you think about the Holy Trinity—the Father, the Son, and the Holy Spirit—consider a man who is a father, a son, and a spouse. He is one and the same, but he has different responsibilities in his various roles. The same is true of God. He is one, yet he reveals himself to us in three ways. As the Father, he has never been seen (John 1:18); as the Son, he has walked among us (John 1:14–18); as the Holy Spirit, he is working within us (John 16:8 and 1 Corinthians 6:19–20).

Record reflections in your journal.

Prayer: As you pray to God, thank him for the Holy Spirit's growing presence in your life. Ask that the Spirit's influence will continue to increase. Ask that you might recognize the gifts that God has given you. Finally, pray for guidance in developing and using those gifts to glorify him.

Journal

Chapter 6

You and your church

A s a Christian, you are a part of both a church and the Church.

Sound confusing? Try this explanation: A church is built by people, but the Church is built of people. A church—with the small letter c—is a bricks-and-mortar (or wood-and-nails) structure that is created to serve as a place of worship. The Church—with the capital C—refers to the people of God. That's why we say that Christians may be part of a church congregation, but on a larger scale, they also are part of the all-inclusive body of Christ.

The Bible paints vivid pictures to help us understand the concept of the Church as the people of God. In 1 Corinthians 12, Paul likens the Church to the human body—a unit made up of many organs and limbs, each contributing its special "gift" to the workings of the whole. "So it is with Christ. For we were all baptized by one Spirit into one body—whether Jews or Greeks, slave or free—and we were all given the one Spirit to drink" (vv 12–13, NIV).

Paul goes on to explain that in the body of Christ, each of us has gifts that contribute to the mission and ministry of the Church. The Church is the body in which Christ lives. Through this body—made up of us, the parts—Jesus continues to carry on his work of saving people throughout the world.

Another illustration is drawn for us in 1 Peter 2:4–10. Here, Jesus is likened to a living stone that was rejected by men but chosen by God. People who have made the commitment to follow Christ are portrayed as stones that collectively take the form of a spiritual house (the Church) and continue the ministry of Jesus. Clearly, followers of Jesus are the chosen people of God. "Once you were not a people, but now you are the people of God; once you had not received mercy, but now you have received mercy" (v 10, NIV).

These passages make the point that the Church is not merely a collection of individuals who join together to pursue a casual interest. This is a group whose members are linked forever by a passionate belief in Christ and a burning desire to bring nonbelievers into the body. Each individual is related, and all cooperate as a unit to carry on the mission of Jesus. The members suffer with those who are in distress and rejoice with those who rejoice.

The intimate relationship between Christ and his Church is underscored in Ephesians 5:29–30: "After all, no one ever hated his own body, but he feeds and cares for it, just as Christ does the Church—for we are members of his body" (NIV). The Church is the object of Christ's love. He feeds it and cares for it, and his presence gives it life.

NO DUES REQUIRED

Membership in the Church is a spiritual experience and is not determined by ceremony or decree. Persons who have met Jesus Christ and have surrendered to the supernatural work of God in the human soul are welcomed into the fellowship. But although membership is available to all, it shouldn't be taken lightly. As a body of redeemed persons, we have certain responsibilities. Among them, we are expected to show:

√ obedience to the God who redeemed us.

√ dedication to the mission of preaching, teaching and witnessing to what God has done for us.

√ willingness to grow in Christ by hearing and studying the word at weekly worship services, entering into ministry with other believers, and helping to further God's kingdom in our home communities.

THE LINK BETWEEN CHURCH AND CHURCH

The idea is profound yet simple. Our effectiveness as Christians is greatly decreased if we try to minister without the support and talents of other members of our group. The new life that we all have found in Christ is realized more fully in fellowship with other Christians. The body of believers is the Church, and these believers find unity and strength in the church.

Stretching Exercises

When you are part of a body of believers, you are a vital participant in an important give-and-take relationship. You support the other members just as they support you. Sometimes you may feel that you receive more than you give, but that can quickly change as situations and needs arise. Think for a moment about the group with whom you worship. Describe the ways in which the members—both individually and collectively—support you.

_____

_____

_____

Now describe your contribution to the group.

_____

_____

_____

According to recent research, many young Christians in the 18-to-30 age group choose not to attend the churches of their childhoods, but visit many congregations until they find the church "home" that meets their needs. Envision the local church of your dreams. How big is it? What kinds of special ministries does it have? Where is its location? How large and specialized is the pastoral staff? How formal is its worship? What kinds of opportunities for growth and participation does it offer the members of its congregation? Try to articulate these characteristics in a few sentences.

_____

_____

_____

_____

_____

Paraphrase this verse from the New Testament: "Now you are the body of Christ and individually members of it" (1 Corinthians 12:27, RSV).

_____

_____

_____

In his book *Hi-Q Christians,* Dr. Oral Withrow lists what each of us can expect from the church we attend and, in return, what the church we attend can expect from each of us. Read the list on the left and then try to create a response list on the right.

What you can expect from the church	**What the church expects from you**
The word of God, proclaimed, taught, made relevant to your life.	_____ _____ _____
The sacraments, administered solemnly and with dignity.	_____ _____
Opportunities to equip yourself for ministry within the church and the community.	_____ _____ _____
Prayer in times of need.	_____
Guidance for life in the form of sermon messages and counseling.	_____ _____

Inclusion in meaningful
groups, both large and small,
within the church.

_____
_____
_____

Friendship.

_____

GROUP DISCUSSION TOPIC

In our very mobile society, "church" is as close as our computer terminals, television sets, radios or CD players. Online "chat" groups enable us to discuss religion with people around the globe. Television preachers, who may be more gifted speakers than our local pastors, can inspire us with stirring rhetoric. We can listen to Christian talk shows on our car radios as we drive to and from the office. We can pop in a compact disc and listen to everything from contemporary gospel music to the great classical oratorios.

With all these resources available to us, why is it essential that we attend a local church on a regular basis?

Respond to these questions:

√ What is the relationship between the church and the denominational bodies we see all around us?

√ How does a person become a member of God's church?

√ Who has authority in and over the church? How is this exhibited?

√ How may the church take on a servant role in the world?

√ What is your best definition of "church?"

MEDITATION

Think about this passage from 1 Peter 2:9: "But you are a chosen race, a royal priesthood, a holy nation, God's own people, that you may declare the wonderful deeds of him who called you out of darkness into his marvelous light" (RSV).

How do the words make you feel? Are you empowered by them? Motivated to take some kind of action?

_____

_____

_____

_____

Journal

Chapter 7

What does
the church believe?

As you take your place in your chosen congregation and in the body of Christ, you will become familiar with the beliefs and practices of both. Many expressions of worship—the type of music played, the length and formality of the service, the level of participation by the members—will vary. But the most basic principles are universal; they serve as the foundation of our Christian faith and are not subject to change. They are our common ground. They are what the church believes. And, as a Christian, you share these beliefs wholeheartedly.

√ The church believes in the existence of God.

Throughout its history, the church has encountered God and witnessed his powerful acts. His strength is indisputable; as creator and ruler, he has total authority over our lives. He is holy and governs the universe with wisdom. We are in awe of who he is and what he does. We respond to him with total respect, love and obedience.

√ The church believes that Christ is the Son of God.

Both human and divine, Jesus Christ became man for our salvation. We speak of this great event—the coming of the Son of God to our world—as the "incarnation." This term means "becoming in flesh" and is in harmony with John 1:14, which states, "the word (Jesus) became flesh." Paul speaks of this as God "sending his own son in the likeness of sinful flesh" (here the word "likeness" means man's appearance, but not that his nature was tainted with sin.—Romans 8:3). By dying on the cross, Christ atoned for our sins.

√ The church believes all people can be saved.

We are assured of this truth in Romans 8:1–11. "There is, therefore, no condemnation." Why? Forgiveness has been granted by God and the guilt of sin has been removed. Paul's great word in the Book of Romans is "justification." It means not only forgiveness and pardon for sins, but also that God at the same time receives us into fellowship with himself and treats us as if we were never sinners. Obstacles are removed, and we have "peace with God through our Lord Jesus Christ" (Romans 5:1).

√ **The church believes in and practices the ordinances.**

In support of its beliefs, the church observes three important symbolic events that were sanctioned by Jesus, reenacted by early Christians and handed down to us to carry on collectively in his name. These events are baptism, which we'll explore in the next chapter; the Lord's Supper, first celebrated on the night before Christ's crucifixion; and foot washing, a poignant reminder of the servant character of the church.

Let's look at the Lord's Supper and foot washing, saving baptism for chapter 8.

√ **The Lord's Supper.** While commemorating the Passover with his followers, Jesus offered them bread and then wine, saying, "This is my body," and "This is my blood" (Mark 14:22–24). The passage in 1 Corinthians 11:23–29, written by the Apostle Paul, shows that this supper was observed regularly in the New Testament church. The church, all through the centuries that followed, has continued the sharing of sacraments. The significance of the Lord's Supper is in the symbols of the bread and the wine, which represent the body and blood of Christ, whose death on the cross was in atonement for man's sin.

√ **Foot washing.** To fully understand the importance of this act, you have to know that the foot symbolizes subjugation in the Bible. In John 13:4–17, Jesus—the model of servanthood throughout his ministry—teaches his disciples an important lesson when he pours water into a basin and washes his disciples' feet and dries them with the towel wrapped around his waist. By repeating this act for members of our own worship group, we acknowledge that we are servants of each other. At the same time, we recall the words of Jesus: "If I then, your Lord and Teacher, have washed your feet, you also ought to wash one another's feet" (v 14, RSV).

√ The church believes that Jesus Christ is coming again.

Throughout the Bible we find many clues that, when pieced together, give us a vivid picture of Christ's second coming. We know his appearance will be very visible and unexpected. Matthew 24:30–31 describes the dramatic moment: "At that time the sign of the Son of Man will appear in the sky, and all the nations of the earth will mourn. They will see the Son of Man coming on the clouds of the sky, with power and great glory. And he will send his angels with a loud trumpet call, and they will gather his elect from the four winds, from one end of the heavens to the other" (NIV). When will all this occur? No date is predicted; only God knows the moment.

We're also told of the dramatic reaction to Christ's second coming. There will be a general resurrection of the dead (Acts 24:15); all nations will be gathered before him (Matthew 25:31–32); and a final judgment will follow (Acts 17:31). The earth, as we know it, will end, but an eternal order will begin. "That day will bring about the destruction of the heavens by fire, and the elements will melt in the heat. But in keeping with his promise we are looking forward to a new heaven and a new earth, the home of righteousness" (2 Peter 3:12–13, NIV). A detailed picture of the "new heaven and new earth" is contained in Revelation 21.

Stretching Exercises

Hebrews 11:6 warns us that "without faith it is impossible to please him. For whoever would draw near to God must believe that he exists and that he rewards those who seek him" (RSV). Why did the writer feel the need to express such an obvious truth? What does this verse mean to you? Try to paraphrase it in your own words.

_____

_____

_____

Create a list of six beliefs related to your Christian faith that you are absolutely certain in your heart are true. How would you explain or defend these beliefs to a doubting friend who demanded "proof?"

_____   _____

_____   _____

_____   _____

_____   _____

Respond to these questions:

What opportunities are available for you to learn more about God, the church and the basic beliefs of the Christian faith?

_____

_____

_____

React to this statement: "It doesn't matter what you believe just so you believe something!"

_____

_____

_____

Do you know anyone who has chosen unworthy or unhealthy beliefs? Have you tried to share your faith?

_____

_____

_____

_____

Among the most powerful scriptures in the New Testament is 1 Corinthians 15:1–8. The resurrection of Jesus from the dead was God's approval upon him, upon who he said he was, and upon what he was able to do. His resurrection means that death has been conquered. Because God raised Jesus from the dead, he is able to raise us also to share in his glory and victory.

As you read these verses, answer these questions in your journal.

How does God's word, as recorded in 1 Corinthians 15:1–8, speak to you?

What adjustments do you believe God wants you to make in your life?

What adjustments have you already made in anticipation of sharing his glory and victory?

Journal

Chapter 8

Christian baptism

Perhaps you are thinking about being baptized.

Perhaps you've never participated in the ritual or, if you have, you want to repeat it as a symbol of your new or renewed faith. You know this is an important observance—a milestone of sorts—that has been part of our Christian tradition since John wandered the desert urging people to first repent and then be baptized. The practice seems to represent a beginning, a clean slate, a commitment to start over, live obediently, and follow Christ's teachings. It's a way to stand up and be counted.

You also know that baptism has God's blessing. You've read in Mark that after Jesus was baptized by John in the Jordan, "he saw heaven being torn open and the Spirit descending on him like a dove. And a voice came from heaven: 'You are my Son, whom I love; with you I am well pleased' " (Mark 1:10–11, NIV).

FIRST COMES REPENTANCE

As important as the ritual of baptism is, salvation is dependent upon an internal relationship with God, not an external act of the church. If no relationship exists, the baptism ceremony is little more than a familiar text that climaxes with a dramatic action. Only when a "rebirth" precedes baptism does the ritual have true meaning. It is a way that believers can testify before a body of witnesses that Christ has come into their hearts, they have repented of their sins, and they are committed to the church's ministry. This public act doesn't automatically make them a part of the church, but it symbolizes their membership in the larger body of believers—the Church. (See chapter 6.)

Jesus emphasizes the importance of baptism when he says in Mark 16:16, "Whoever believes and is baptized will be saved, but whoever does not believe will be condemned" (NIV). Notice the order that he specifies: First you believe, then you are baptized. Only those who believe are assured of salvation.

Baptism takes on even more significance when Christ includes it as part of the Great Commission that he gives his disciples at the end of his ministry on earth. The last words in the Book of Matthew tell his followers to "go and make disciples of all nations, baptizing them in the name of the Father and of the Son and of the Holy Spirit, and teaching them to obey everything I have commanded you. And surely I am with you always, to the very end of the age" (Matthew 28:19–20, NIV).

The Book of Acts contains many examples of how the disciples obeyed Christ's order. Consider:

√ Peter telling the crowd to "repent and be baptized every one of you in the name of Jesus Christ" (Acts 2:38).

√ Philip baptizing the Ethiopian by the side of the road (Acts 8:30–38).

√ Ananias healing Saul's eyes and then baptizing him (Acts 9:18).

WHAT HAPPENS ON MONDAY MORNING?

If baptism is a milestone, believers can anticipate many more milestones as they continue their Christian journey. We're told to "make every effort to supplement your faith with virtue, and virtue with knowledge, and knowledge with self-control, and self-control with steadfastness, and steadfastness with godliness, and godliness with brotherly affection, and brotherly affection with love" (2 Peter 1:5–7, RSV). As you look beyond baptism and ahead to your heightened commitment to Christ, you might consider three opportunities to pursue:

√ Get involved more fully in the life of the church. Make a list of the ways you now participate; make a list of ways you might expand that participation.

√ Revisit the Book of Acts and note how the followers of Christ took advantage of every opportunity to share the gospel. How often do you witness? Perhaps it's time to offer your testimony more frequently.

√ Step up your study of the Bible. To grow spiritually, you must increase your knowledge of the scriptures. Growing Christians are Bible Christians.

Stretching Exercises

Some churches practice the baptism of infants. Other churches "dedicate" babies and baptize adults. If baptism is symbolic of belief and commitment, at what point in life does the ceremony seem most appropriate? Support your response with examples from the Bible.

_____

_____

_____

Think about your own baptism experience. How did you prepare for it? How did you feel before the ceremony? After the ceremony? Were you changed in any way? Was the decision to be baptized a part of a larger commitment? Have you been able to sustain the commitment?

_____

_____

_____

Depending on church tradition, the ordinance of baptism may involve the sprinkling of water on the forehead or the immersion of the entire body in a baptismal pool. (Baptize comes from the Greek word _baptizo,_ which means to dip, plunge, or immerse.) What argument might support the practice of immersion?

_____

_____

_____

Membership in the church doesn't depend on any formal act of confirmation. Yet in 1 Corinthians 12:13, Paul tells us that "by one Spirit are we all baptized into one body." What is the difference between baptism in water and baptism of the Spirit?

_____

_____

Respond to these questions:

√ The church regularly engages in three symbolic rites—communion, foot washing, and baptism. What value do these ordinances have for Christians?

_____

_____

√ How does an "ordinance" differ from a "sacrament?"

_____

_____

√ What might cause a person to be baptized more than once?

_____

_____

_____

√ Baptism offers a promise: "Repent, and be baptized every one of you in the name of Jesus Christ for the forgiveness of your sins; and you shall receive the gift of the Holy Spirit" (Acts 2:38, RSV). What does the "gift of the Holy Spirit" mean to you? Review chapter 5 before you respond.

_____

_____

_____

Journal opportunity

Put yourself into this verse (Romans 6:4): "(I was) buried therefore with him by baptism into death, so that as Christ was raised from the dead by the glory of the Father, (I) too might walk in newness of life" (RSV). What does this mean to you? How does it make you feel? Encouraged? Obligated to make changes in your life? Think about it, then put your thoughts on paper.

Journal

Journal

Chapter 9

Stewardship

W here do *you* draw the line?

One of the most painful confrontations in the New Testament involves a wealthy young man who begs Jesus to tell him how he might enter the kingdom of God. "Follow the Ten Commandments," answers Christ, listing the familiar laws set forth by God.

"Easy enough," assures the youth. "I've followed those rules all my life."

Then Christ takes one step beyond and asks the impossible: "Go, sell everything you have and give it to the poor, and you will have treasure in heaven. Then come, follow me." The young man weighs his options—worldly wealth vs. eternal life—and makes his choice. Wealth wins. The man draws the line when it comes to forfeiting his money. He simply cannot let go of what he views as his personal property. He hasn't grasped the concept that God is the owner of all things, and that we are responsible to hold in God's name whatever gifts or possessions come into our care and keeping. Simply put: Nothing is really ours.

"It is easier for a camel to go through the eye of a needle than for a rich man to enter the kingdom of God," remarks Jesus to his disciples as they watch the young man walk away.

CHOOSING A SERVANT LIFESTYLE

The Bible constantly reminds us that the earth and everything in it belongs not to us, but to God. The Old Testament explains, "Every beast of the forest is mine ... the world and all that is in it is mine" (Psalm 50:10–12, RSV). The New Testament expands the same thought, "Whether we live or whether we die, we are the Lord's" (Romans 14:8, RSV).

Our task on earth—clearly spelled out in scripture—is to act as stewards (agents, custodians, overseers) of God's world. What's more, the amount of responsibility that God expects us to assume is directly related to our ability and our wealth. "From everyone who has been given much, much will be demanded; and from the one who has been entrusted with much, much more will be asked" (Luke 12:48, NIV).

If we think of ourselves as custodians of God's world, we also must understand that at some point we will be held responsible for what we have done or haven't done. Our work will be evaluated. "Each of us will give an account of himself to God" (Romans 14:12, NIV).

The modern dilemma, of course, is how do we share our wealth? Good causes abound. The world and its people have so many needs. How much do we give? How do we balance our responsibilities to our families, our communities and God's world? The Bible offers many guidelines. Among them:

√ A tithe (one tenth) of everything from the land, whether grain from the soil or fruit from the trees, belongs to the Lord.
(Leviticus 27:30, NIV)

√ When you give to the needy, do not announce it with trumpets.
(Matthew 6:2, NIV)

√ Freely you have received, freely give. Do not take along any gold or silver or copper in your belts; take no bag for the journey, or extra tunic, or sandals or a staff; for the worker is worth his keep.
(Matthew 10:8–10, NIV)

√ Each man should give what he has decided in his heart to give, not reluctantly or under compulsion, for God loves a cheerful giver.
(2 Corinthians 9:7, NIV)

Stretching Exercises

One of the best known verses of scripture warns that "the love of money is the root of all evil" (1 Timothy 6:10, KJV). The text goes on to explain that, "Some people, eager for money, have wandered from the faith and pierced themselves with many griefs" (v 10, NIV). What does this passage say to you? Is wealth a burden? A challenge? Something to pursue? Shun?

_____

_____

_____

God's gifts are not limited to financial wealth. When we think about being good stewards of the Lord's possessions, we must think of the environment and everything in it. (Review Genesis 1:28 and Psalm 8:5–8.) To truly follow a "servant lifestyle," what changes would you need to make?

_____

_____

_____

In chapter 5 we explored the idea that God gives each of us special gifts to use in spreading the gospel of Jesus Christ. With that thought in mind, consider this passage from 1 Peter 4:10, "As each has received a gift, employ it for one another, as good stewards of God's varied grace." How might we use our gifts to help one another?

_____

_____

_____

Respond to these questions:

√ How might stewardship relate to pursuing volunteer opportunities in your community?

_____

_____

√ A popular expression of a few years ago urged us to "look out for No. 1." How would Jesus view this mindset? Review the Bible's teachings on selfishness and greed.

_____

_____

√ What are the guidelines for giving as set forth in the Bible?

_____

_____

√ Explain the concept of man having been created to have dominion over God's world. What are the limits of our responsibilities? How much control are we expected to have in reality?

_____

_____

Journal

Chapter 10

Witnessing:
passing the faith along

Who *me?* you might ask.

Yes, *you.*

Every follower of Christ—even a new believer such as yourself—has received an assignment so important that it is known throughout the Christian world as the Great Commission. Described in various ways in the New Testament, this "order" is spelled out most clearly in Mark 16:15, "Go into all the world and preach the good news to all creation" (NIV). Another version, this one found in Acts 1:8, offers assurance that God will help you carry out the task, "You will receive power when the Holy Spirit comes on you; and you will be my witnesses in Jerusalem ... and to the ends of the earth" (NIV).

Some people call it the principle of spiritual multiplication or, more simply, "passing the faith along." Paul explains the concept to his young friend, Timothy, this way: "The things you have heard me say in the presence of many witnesses entrust to reliable men who will also be qualified to teach others" (2 Timothy 2:2, NIV). Jesus, the master teacher, modeled how to do it. Without benefit of mass media or sophisticated technology he managed to bring the message of God's salvation to the world by concentrating his training on twelve men. These men, in turn, trained others. At some point, someone—parents, friends, Sunday school teacher, pastor—passed the faith to you.

Now it's your turn. At the very heart of being a Christian are two responsibilities: the responsibility to be a disciple yourself, and the responsibility "to disciple"—to lead—others into this role.

A WORK IN PROGRESS

Frightened by the challenge? Think you're too new to the faith? Haven't felt the "call" yet? Doubt your ability to lead anyone to Christ because you're still a newcomer yourself?

The good news is that you have many ways to be a witness for Christ. One of the most common is to share your testimony with a friend. This can be a simple one-on-one account of your relationship with Jesus. It can be a brief expression of your own experience, of where you have been and how you arrived at this point in your Christian pilgrimage. You can explain that you are a "work in progress," and that you can only speak to where Christ has brought you today.

Another way to witness is by your actions. Old habits may fall away as you start to stretch and grow under God's loving guidance. You are no longer the same person, and the changes may be evident.

Stretching Exercises

The Bible contains several personal stories that can serve as models as you think about sharing your testimony with other people. In Acts 22:1–16, Paul quiets an angry mob with his story of how he became a Christian. First he establishes common ground with the crowd ("I am a Jew ... brought up in this city ... trained in the law of our fathers"), then he admits to making many mistakes in his life, and finally he recalls the encounter with Jesus that led to his baptism.

Not everyone's story is as dramatic or as dangerous as Paul's. Still, all testimonies have similar characteristics. They are one-of-a-kind, eyewitness accounts of personal experiences that happen to people just like us. And because they continue to happen over and over again in our times and to our neighbors, they are constant reminders of Christ's relevance in this day and age. They stand as contemporary translations of what he can do in our lives right now.

Begin to organize your testimony by responding to these prompts:

√ Describe your life before you became a Christian.

_____

_____

_____

√ Recall the moment you realized that you wanted and needed Jesus Christ in your life.

_____

_____

_____

√ Tell how you asked for and received Jesus Christ.

_____

_____

_____

√ Explain how your life has changed since you became a Christian.

_____

_____

_____

Compare the different versions of Paul's testimony in Acts 9:1–19, Acts 22:1–16, and Galatians 1:11–17. Although the facts are the same, descriptions and details vary. Now, think about your own testimony.

√ How might you tell your story differently if you were talking with a preteen? A small group of same-gender friends? A large mixed gathering of adults whom you had never met before? A skeptic who showed no interest in spiritual matters?

√ What aspects of your testimony might you choose to emphasize or omit depending on your audience? Why? How would you compact your story into two minutes if that was all the time you had to reach someone?

Jesus has told us to make disciples of all nations, baptize new believers and teach them about the Father, Son, and Holy Spirit. How can you follow this commission if you are tethered to a 9-to-5 job or are a stay-at-home mom responsible for young children?

Second Corinthians 3:2–3 says: "You yourselves are our letter, written on our hearts, known and read by everybody. You show that you are a letter from Christ, the result of our ministry, written not with ink but with the Spirit of the living God, not on tablets of stone but on tablets of human hearts" (NIV).

What does this passage mean to you? Try to paraphrase it.

_____

_____

_____

Which do you think comes first—words or deeds? Which is more important? Is there a way to balance the two?

List four ways you can fulfill the Great Commission and "pass the faith along" without leaving your community.

1. _____   3. _____

2. _____   4. _____

If you are interested in exploring further any one of these topics, Warner Press offers a series of helpful books under the series title BRIDGES: INVITATION TO DISCIPLESHIP—First and Last Things: The Certainty of Eternal Life (D5301); The Bible: Our Guide for Daily Living (D5302); Prayer: An Enjoyable Experience (D5303); The Holy Spirit: Power to Be Like Jesus (D5304); The People of God: Identifying the Church (D5305); Temptations: Victory Over Persistent Problems (D5310); Telling Others: A Witnessing Lifestyle (D5308); Jesus: Savior and Lord (D5307); and Stewardship: Whole Life Discipleship (D5306). Call 1–800–741–7721 and order by code and title.

Journal